SETTLERS UNDER SAIL

DON CHARLWOOD

Don Charlwood

Burgewood Books
Melbourne

Burgewood Books
4 Diane Court,
Warrandyte,
Victoria 3113
Australia

First Published 1978
Reprinted 1981
Second edition 1991
Third edition 1999
ISBN 1 876425 06 7

Printed and bound in Malaysia through
SRM Production Services Sdn. Bhd.

FOREWORD

In 1975 the then Premier, Sir Rupert Hamer, K.C.M.G., established the History Advisory Council of Victoria. The purpose of this council was to advise the Government as to which historical events should be celebrated or commemorated, by whom, when, where, together with a budget estimate of cost. It was intended to bring to the people history in a form which would be not only exciting but which would involve many citizens and be readily assimilated by the community at large. It was my privilege to have been appointed the inaugural Chairman.

One such series of events was wrecks on the south coast with the focal point being the commemoration of the centenary of the wreck of the vessel "Loch Ard" on June 1, 1878. In this series were several components, including displays at the Maritime Museum in Warrnambool, rescue operations in Port Campbell inlet and a most dramatic ceremony in the Loch Ard Gorge at 5.45am on June 4 1978 on a chill winter's morning.

The interest of the public was such that approximately 2,000 people actually descended into the gorge for the service and a grilled sausage, bacon, coffee and rum breakfast. It was a most dignified and spine tingling service in which the author of *Settlers Under Sail,* Mr Don Charlwood, delivered a splendid address from an elevated position on the side of the cliff. He spoke as well as he writes.

Mr Charlwood, who was an active member of the organising committee, was persuaded at one of the early meetings to write a brief history of wrecks on the Victorian coast. These wrecks, of course, featured very prominently in our early history. The admirable title *Settlers Under Sail* was chosen. It was researched so thoroughly and written in such a graphic style that it not only enthralled its readers but achieved wide publicity for our commemoration and brought great credit to both the author and organisers.

I remember well Mr Charlwood's first book, *No Moon Tonight,* in which he so graphically captured the atmosphere of a Lancaster bomber participating in a World War II raid over Germany. The quality of *Settlers Under Sail* is equivalent and is such that a further edition of it is fully justified.

I feel confident that readers will not only enjoy the reading but be very much better informed about a most important aspect of our early history.

Sir John Holland, A.C.

Other books by Don Charlwood

No Moon Tonight
All the Green Year
An Afternoon of Time
Take-off to Touchdown
The Wreck of the Loch Ard
Wrecks and Reputations
Flight and Time
The Long Farewell
Marching as to War
Journeys Into Night

Contents

"The concussion was alarmingly loud, and all was confusion and terror"—
a contemporary etching of the Loch Ard*'s last moments.*

*A*t approximately 5 o'clock on the morning of June 1, 1878, the clipper *Loch Ard,* approaching the western entrance to Bass Strait in thick mist, ran onto a reef off Mutton Bird Island, 27 miles northwest of Cape Otway. She sank quickly, only 120 yards from the precipitous mainland coast.

Seventeen of her 18 passengers went down with the ship or were drowned soon afterwards. The one surviving passenger, Eva Carmichael, a girl of 18, clung to a spar and was washed into a deep gorge. She was rescued there by the one survivor of the crew, Tom Pearce, an 18-year-old apprentice.

In all, 52 people lost their lives. Eva Carmichael lost not only her parents, but her five brothers and sisters.

A loss of this magnitude, so close to Melbourne, and the drama of Eva Carmichael's rescue, moved the Australian people deeply. But one aspect of the tragedy was beyond seeing for several years: the 17 passengers drowned that morning were to be the last of many emigrants lost when a sailing ship failed to negotiate the western entrance to Bass Strait. There were to be later sailing ship tragedies at the entrance, but not another involving emigrant lives.

Without Victorians of the time being aware of it, the era of immigration by sailing ship was drawing to its close.

It is impossible, of course, to put a precise date to the era's end. Steamships and steam-assisted auxiliaries had been carrying the bulk of emigrants before the wreck of the *Loch Ard,* and a trickle continued to come by sail after the wreck. But this one dramatic event highlights the last days of immigration under sail.

SETTLERS UNDER SAIL

The Realities of Sail

*T*he sailing ship was undoubtedly one of humanity's most noble creations, but even in skilled hands it was at the mercy of the wind. Masters dreaded being pinned to a lee shore, since escape by sailing into the eye of the wind was impossible. And when the Gold Rush emigrants led shipping companies to provide faster and faster passages, the risks of sail were increased. The western entrance to Bass Strait alone was to see 18 ships lost at the end of long voyages.

The western entrance lies between Cape Otway in Victoria and Cape Wickham, the northernmost point of King Island. The two are 55 miles apart. To the layman of today this seems ample distance for safe passage of flotillas of ships, but one has also to take into account the long journey without sight of land that many of these ships had made.

In the early years of the New South Wales settlement it was not known that Bass Strait existed. It was generally supposed that Van Diemen's Land was part of the mainland. But in 1798 Bass and Flinders, sailing out of Sydney, entered the strait from the east and, continuing their voyage, circumnavigated Van Diemen's Land. Although they had proved existence of a strait, they did not sight any part of the western entrance, for they were clinging to the Van Diemen's Land coast in their task of circumnavigation.

The prospect of using the newly-discovered strait to cut 700 miles off the distance from Britain to Sydney immediately interested the British Admiralty. In 1800 they instructed Lieutenant James Grant, Sydney-bound in the *Lady Nelson*, to attempt the strait from the west. Grant did so. He named the great downward thrust of Victoria,

Cape Albany Otway. But even he did not know the width of the entrance. Hugging the mainland coast as he was, he did not sight King Island. The width of the entrance would not in any event have troubled him, for unlike the giant sailing ships that were some day to follow him, he was proceeding very cautiously, having no reason to make a fast passage.

King Island was named in the following month by the second master to pass through Bass Strait from the west—Captain Black in the *Harbinger*. The *Harbinger*'s name was given to extensive reefs that lie off the northern tip of the island, reefs destined to claim many ships in the years ahead.

The strait was soon regarded by the Admiralty as the main approach to eastern Australia. The ships that began using it were mainly convict

"Tea water—soup time"—the Illustrated London News. *In 1842 each passenger was given a weekly ration of seven pounds of bread, biscuit, flour, oatmeal, or rice, or the equivalent in potatoes. Anything more had to be provided by the passengers themselves.*

transports and supply ships, none of them pressed for rapid passages, none of them carrying the vast areas of sail that were to come later.

It is extraordinary to consider that in more than 800 sailings of convict transports to Australia, only four were lost by shipwreck. One of these four occurred at the western entrance to Bass Strait in 1835, a month before Batman arrived in Port Phillip. The transport *Neva*, bringing a wretched shipment of convict women and their children from Cork, was lost on the Harbinger Reefs trying to enter the strait. Of her complement of 241, only 22 reached shore; of these, seven died on the beach.

Although this disaster pointed to the need for a landfall lighthouse, the Cape Otway area was still *terra incognita* from the landward side and known only to whalers and sealers from the seaward side. It was to be three more years before Superintendent La Trobe was appointed to the new settlement on the Yarra.

The firstcomers to Melbourne were from Van Diemen's Land and Sydney, but on Sunday October 27, 1839 the immigrant ship direct from Britain arrived in Hobson's Bay. She was the *David Clark* bearing 229 government-assisted immigrants who had embarked at Greenock four and a half months earlier. The "Port Phillip Patriot and Melbourne Advertiser", under a heading, "Advance Australia Felix", tells us that the *David Clark* carried "industrious labourers of both sexes and before they are well settled, the second vessel direct will have arrived at this port."

In the year that these first immigrant ships arrived, the pilot service at Port Phillip Heads was established. Thirty-seven years before this, no less a navigator than Matthew Flinders had marked warning on his chart of the entrance to the bay: "strong tide ripplings" and the *Investigator* herself had "stuck fast" on a mud bank not far inside. Thus it was clear from the beginning that ships strange to the port would require expert guidance through these waters. By the end of immigration by sail, passengers of only two ships inbound from Britain had lost their lives at the Heads: eleven from *Isabella*

Watson in 1852, and one from the *Columbine* in 1854. When it is considered how many thousands of passengers were arriving annually, the record is a remarkable one.

Emigration to Victoria by sail was to continue for the next 40 years. Auxiliary, or steam-assisted sailing ships, developed over much the same period. By the end of the era, steam ships had taken over passenger carrying except for those few passengers whose preference remained with tall white ships and the freedom they offered from smoke and coal dust.

Unlike emigration to Australia following the Second World War, a great majority of early newcomers were from the British Isles. In 1881 the birthplaces of nearly a million Australian residents were England, Ireland, Scotland, or Wales. The next group numerically was German-born: totalling 42,203. But by the time of this

"Dinner in the forecastle"—an etching from the Illustrated London News, *gives an idea of conditions for steerage passengers on emigrant ships of the period.*

Migration to Australia during the nineteenth century—a contemporary etching of steerage passenger conditions, from the Illustrated London News. *At sea the prevailing British class system continued. Until the coming of Caroline Chisholm, few people queried the fact that saloon passengers lived in relative comfort, with ample food, and were waited upon, while steerage passengers fended for themselves.*

census, Australian-born people exceeded all immigrants by more than 700,000.

The passage times of most of the early ships were wearyingly slow. Shipboard life became a world within a world, shut off from the rest of humanity. Departure from those at home was trial enough, for it was generally accepted as lifelong separation. In June 1839 Mrs Charles Meredith wrote in her journal on board the *Letita:*

I do not know one thing that I felt so much as the loss of the North Star. Night after night I watched it, sinking lower—lower; the well-known "Great Bear" that I had so gazed on even from a child, that it seemed like the face of an old friend, was fast going too; it was like parting from my own loved home-faces over again ... Who might say that we should ever meet again? Those stars seemed like a last link uniting us.

The most consoling events on the run south were chance meetings with home-bound ships. After the masters had compared latitude and longitude, shouting through megaphones, and had exchanged whatever brief, stale news they might have, passengers would despatch through the other captain letters and diaries to their distant families. Many a passenger was illiterate—indeed, even as late as 1851, scarcely more than a quarter of Melbourne's population could write. The illiterates could only dictate hasty letters to those willing to transcribe for them.

Steerage passengers, drawn from the poorer classes, formed by far the largest groups on ships. Although Britain was rising to the peak of her power as leader of the industrial world, the common people were passing through appalling hardships. Drawn from the villages to the great factory centres to find work, thousands of English people lived and worked in conditions that sapped their strength and left them with little hope for a better future. In the Scottish Highlands the situation was as bad, if not worse, but for a different reason: the landowners were clearing villagers out, often forcing them to emigrate, so that the land could be used for vast sheep runs. The common people of Ireland were in an even more impoverished state and, after the potato famines of the 1840s and the typhus that followed them, the people emigrated in a state of panic.

Two things must be remembered about the poorer emigrants: because they had been accustomed to great hardship, they were able to tolerate conditions on the voyage out that today seem intolerable; secondly, harsh though their lives had been, very few of them were happy to leave home.

At sea the prevailing British class system continued. Until the coming of Caroline Chisholm few people queried the fact that saloon passengers lived in relative comfort, with ample food, and were waited upon, while steerage passengers, packed in together, fended for

themselves. Split into "messes" of anything from half a dozen to twenty, each member of the mess took a turn to collect rations and prepare dishes for cooking.

The British Passenger Acts were slow in easing the deplorable steerage conditions. In 1842 each passenger was given a weekly ration of seven pounds of bread, biscuit, flour, oatmeal, or rice, or the equivalent in potatoes. Anything more than this the emigrant had to provide for him- or herself.

Shared sleeping berths for four people were at first a mere 6 feet square and the people sharing them were often strangers to one another.

A full ten years passed before berths were divided in two by a plank so that each couple—husband and wife, two men or two women—had a little privacy in the 3 feet of width shared between them.

It was close proximity indeed, if one's bunk mate proved to be infested with lice, as often happened. If there was one typhus case on board, lice carried it to others.

Emigrants filling in time during calm weather, when they were allowed on deck—or part of it.

Emigration in the 1840s was in the hands of private shipowners, many of whom saw it as a way to quick fortune. It was possible for owners to buy a small, poorly-found ship, insure it well and overload it with emigrants. Even if the ship sank during the voyage out, they stood to make substantial gains. Such tubs were deservedly dubbed "coffin ships".

Basil Lubbock, an authority on the years of sail, wrote of sea travel in the forties: "The horrors of the long five-months passage for the miserable landsmen cooped-up in low, ill-ventilated and overcrowded 'tween decks were fit to be compared with those of the convict ships."

Their losses through disease, malnutrition and shipwreck were, in fact, worse than the record of convict ships. For all their horrors, convict ships at least had a discipline that ensured exercise and food distribution. Steerage passengers, on the other hand, had to prepare their meals for themselves, and were often unable through seasickness to do so. Then, says Lubbock, "the strongest maintained the upper hand over the weakest, and it was even said that there were women who died of starvation."

This was revealed during a government enquiry into the early conditions of emigration. The enquiry established further:

"After many trials to get forward, we came to the decision, however unwillingly, that we were beaten and must return"—Superintendent La Trobe's journal describing his second Otway expedition. The third reached Cape Otway in April 1846.

*"Passed the most miserable night of my life . . ."
Henry Allan's diary, winter 1846, written in the
Otway Forest. This 1891 photograph shows the
density of the forest.*

*. . . that in many cases (the passengers)
would not go on deck, their health suffered
so much that their strength was gone, and
they had not the power to help themselves.
Hence the between decks was like a
loathsome dungeon. When the hatchways
were opened, under which the people were
stowed, the steam rose and the stench was
like that from a pen of pigs.*

Deaths occurred with depressing frequency, often
leaving a widow or widower journeying on to the
new land with dependent children. But more
frequently it was the infant children who died,
deprived as they were of proper diet.

It is not surprising that most emigrants from
Britain in the 1840s went to America. Not that
Atlantic travelling conditions were any better
than those prevailing on the Australian run, but
distance and fares being much less, emigrants

could cling to some hope of returning home.
Australia was frighteningly remote; a place to be
associated with felons. Not until the end of the
forties did the total number of free immigrants in
Australia out-number the total number of
convicts.

In 1845 a group of 370 selected British emigrants
boarded the *Cataraqui* for Melbourne. She
approached the Western Entrance of Bass Strait
on the night of the 3rd August, running before a
westerly gale. With no lighthouse of any kind
existing to guide her, she struck the west coast of
King Island. Of 408 souls, only nine survived.

On receiving news of this disaster the Admiralty
wrote:

> *Each year has been marked by more or
> less loss of life, and the last mail from
> Sydney adds to the catalogue an account
> of the wreck of the* Cataraqui *... My lords
> will consider it their duty to prevent
> transports with troops or convicts to
> attempt navigating the said straits till
> lighthouses have been built and they would
> recommend that emigrant ships also be
> prohibited from navigating them for the
> same period.*

Pressure was now strongly on La Trobe to find a
way to Cape Otway. If emigration to Melbourne
was to continue, safety must be brought to Bass
Strait. Cape Otway had long been recognised as
the place for a lighthouse but no one had yet
reached there by land.

La Trobe went himself to the infant settlement of
Colac and led a party into the forest. It proved
barely penetrable; not only this, it clad ranges
that were too precipitous for horses.

On two occasions in 1845, La Trobe turned back
defeated. In 1846 he tried approaching the cape
from the west. On that side he found the forest to
be broken by much open country, but the terrain
was in places worse than he had previously
encountered. Nevertheless, he reached the cape
and determined the site for a lighthouse. But he
knew that a road to Cape Otway could not
possibly cross the route he had followed.

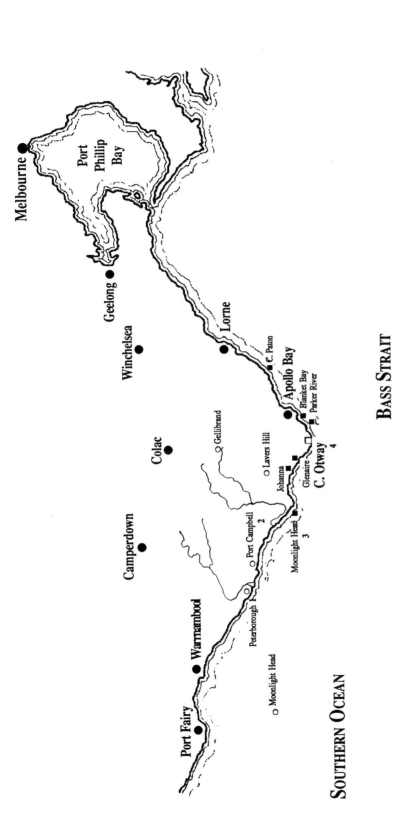

BASS STRAIT

SOUTHERN OCEAN

Principal shipwrecks at the western entrance to Bass Strait (1835-1880)

1. Schomberg	1855	8. Arrow	1865
2. Loch Ard	1878	9. Waterwitch	1854
3. Marie Gabrielle	1869	10. Blencathra	1875
4. Eric The Red	1880	11. Netherby	1866
5. Neva	1835	12. British Admiral	1874
6. Rebecca	1843	13. Cataraqui	1845
7. Brahmin	1854		

"The eye of the needle" entrance to Bass Strait, often negotiated by ships after months without sight of land.
(Map by Creative Solutions)

The coastline from the westward, by which I reached the Cape on foot, however open as far as Moonlight Head, is totally impracticable for horses or oxen beyond that headland. The precipitous and rugged character of the rocky spurs of the mountains abutting upon the straits, and the depth of the wooded ravines which must be passed in attempting to cross them, form serious impediments to approach in any manner. I fear from all I ascertain that approach along the eastern coast will be found equally impracticable. From the westward the Cape is equally unapproachable by sea. In sixty miles of coast in that direction there is certainly no more than one boat harbor and that so far from the Cape as to be useless.

The one boat harbor is today Port Campbell; it lies well over thirty miles by sea from Cape Otway. It was clear to La Trobe that, despite his two earlier failures, a route from near Colac must by some means be established. He nominated "Mr Allan of the Hopkins" as leader of a third exploring party.

Allan made a most strenuous effort. From Colac he crossed the ranges to the present site of Forrest, then headed south to Mt Sabine, from where he dropped steeply through dense forest to Apollo Bay. From there he paralleled the coast where it runs out towards the cape. Heavy, prolonged rain not only delayed them but caused flooding of the short, vigorous rivers lying between his party and their goal.

On June 4th, 1846, La Trobe was obliged to inform the Colonial Secretary in Sydney of Allan's failure:

the party appointed . . . to seek a line of road accessible to horses and oxen from the Colac District, have finally returned to the Border Police Station, after being out from first to last thirty-two days, without having succeeded.

But he was able to add that Allan's party had blazed "a tolerable road" to within five or six miles of the cape.

Late that winter, William Roadknight, a settler from the Geelong district, followed Allan's "tolerable road" and was able to press on over the remaining distance. He not only reached Cape Otway, but followed the coast northwest to take up land beyond the Aire River. He called the property *Glenaire.*

La Trobe quickly reported this success to Sydney, also the fact that surveyor George Smythe had made a detailed survey of the cape from the sea, and had determined a landing place for materials and stores at the mouth of the Parker River.

It was now possible for construction of a lighthouse to begin.

In October, 1846, the tender of Alexander McGillivray was accepted and work was begun. The first attempt failed. The government foreclosed and took over construction. In November 1847, they sent two men overland with bullock drays, following the "tolerable road". At about the same time a working party of forty-three tradesmen left Geelong in the schooner *Teazer*. Although the master of the *Teazer* drowned in his efforts to find a landing place, the party was disembarked on the inhospitable shore and construction of the lighthouse was begun. The shaft was to be only sixty-two feet high, since the cliffs rose to nearly 240 feet. Construction was of sandstone quarried at the Parker River three miles to the east, and drawn to the site in bullock drays.

Nine months later the lantern—"manufactured by Mr Wilkins of London who made the lantern in use in Eddystone lighthouse"—was delivered by one of Benjamin Boyd's ships and landed through the surf.

It was lighted on 29th August, 1848, the second lighthouse on the mainland coast of Australia. In it were twenty-one parabolic reflectors, each with its own wick lamp burning sperm oil, the whole rotated by clockwork, giving a single flash lasting three seconds in every fifty-three.

Sight of the new Otway light by night, or of the white shaft by day, must have brought reassurance not only to ships' masters, but to hundreds of emigrants as well. Behind it reared untamed ranges and forests of giant trees; it faced a treacherous sea, but its presence showed them that men had gone before them, blazing entry to the new land.

During the lighthouse's first year of operation a head keeper was appointed who was to prove the personification of Otway: Henry Bayles Ford, a merchant captain aged 30, appointed at a salary of £120 a year. "My family consists of my wife and two small children, one seven years old, the other two years." Together they were to remain at Cape Otway for thirty years, and there four more Ford children were born. One of the sons was destined to play a part in the rescue operations following the wreck of the *Loch Ard.*

We cannot even guess how many emigrant lives were saved by the presence of the Otway lighthouse. Masters relied on it heavily, for it was usually their first landfall at the end of the 7000 mile run from the Cape of Good Hope. And a time was coming when the call at Cape Town would be cut out; when "The Otway" would often be the first sighting after leaving Britain.

In 1851 the reluctance of Britons to emigrate to Australia suddenly changed. Discovery of gold in Victoria set thousands clamoring to reach the colony as quickly as possible, not only from Britain, but from all countries. Strong competition between shipping companies ensured the largest profits going to those with the fastest ships.

Beautiful wooden ships were built on yacht-like lines, their raked masts sometimes rising higher than 200 feet. They carried sail that could be reckoned by the acre, sometimes as many as three acres. The best of them came at first from American yards. In the hands of a resolute master these ships took advantage of nearly every wind that blew. The names of ships and masters became household words.

But by what route to Australia did the fastest passage lie and where did the strongest winds blow?

The answer to both questions was the same: on the great circle through the Southern Indian Ocean, a sea until then known only to explorers and whalers. It had long been recognised that the shortest distance between any two points on the globe lies along the shorter arc of the great circle joining them. But the true great circle route linking Europe to Australia crosses part of the Antarctic continent, consequently a compromise had to be reached: masters were directed to sail as close to the great circle as ice and the state of the ship allowed. This route became known as the "composite great circle".

Sailing the Great Circle Route

*A*n essential instrument for mariners attempting this route was a reliable chronometer which would remain accurate despite the movements of the ship. Ships' chronometers remained set on Greenwich Mean Time throughout a voyage.

Provided the navigating officer could see the sun reach its zenith each noon, he could determine by how many hours local noon differed from Greenwich time. Each hour of difference represented 15° away from Greenwich. Thus he determined his longitude. The same sun sight, by reference to tables, provided latitude.

Henry Bayles Ford, head keeper of Cape Otway lighthouse for thirty years: 1848– 78. 'There is no record of any failings of the Light since it has been in my charge . . .'

Rare photographs taken aboard sailing ships during the late 1890s and early 1900s.

Aboard the Loch Broom *circa 1890 or earlier.*

The sailing ship Monkbarnes *in heavy weather in 1910.*

Cape Otway lighthouse,
built 1846-1848.
"My Lords will consider it their duty
to prevent transports with troops or
with convicts to attempt navigating
the said straits till lighthouses have
been built, and they would
recommend that emigrant ships
should also be prohibited from
navigating them for the same
period"—Admiralty, 1846.

Chronometers had been extremely expensive in Cook's day, but by the time of the Victorian gold rush, an English watchmaker, John Towson, had produced a small, cheap model. Towson was also examiner of ships' masters at Liverpool, and he urged each master going to Australia to follow the composite great circle. Astonishingly short passage times began to result from these methods.

Masters no longer confined themselves to the Roaring Forties, familiar to them on the run from Cape Town to Cape Otway; they passed in fact 800 miles south of Cape Town and 800 miles south of Cape Leeuwin; they were in latitude 50° south, even 55°, in seas and winds that swept unimpeded around the world.

At best they might sight a few remote islands, at worst nothing but drifting icebergs until they were obliged to thread the needle's eye between Otway and the unmarked Cape Wickham.

One of the most vivid descriptions of sailing the composite great circle to Australia was written by William Scoresby, sea captain, clergyman, and authority on ships' compasses. In 1856, at the age of 67, he came to Melbourne on the auxiliary ship *Royal Charter*.

Far south in the Indian Ocean he wrote that, not even in accounts of hurricanes which he had often read, did the sea "gain the enormous height it now had with us—a height frequently of forty feet—regular waves rolling in the direction of the wind and incomparably higher peaks and crests produced by crossing waves."

The wind was so strong that it not only blew off the crests of the waves, but actually "seized upon great masses of the roaring peaks—cut them off—and drifted them away. Thus the quantity of drift (was) so dense that vision was limited in all directions to about the third part of a mile."

He records seeing four men at the helm, "keeping the wheel in active play as they endeavoured to counteract any sideway tendency of the ship's head"; behind them a "mountain-like wave threatening to overwhelm the ship."

If such an experienced captain, a man who had carried out exploratory work in Icelandic waters, was so awed by the conditions, the feelings of hundreds of emigrants battened below may be imagined. Steerage passengers' conditions over the past decade had improved little. Meat, potatoes and peas had been added to their diet, indeed it was now possible to exist—but only just—without bringing supplementary food of one's own.

Supervision had improved, matrons being provided for the unmarried women, and a surgeon superintendent with overall responsibility for passengers' welfare. Steerage passengers generally represented double the number of all other classes. Few of them had ever been to sea; fewer would ever wish to go again. All too many were inadequately clad, either because of poverty, or because they assumed that 50° to 55° south would be much the same climatically as its equivalent in the northern hemisphere. London, Birmingham, Sheffield and Newcastle were all in that band of northern latitudes, but they were warmed by the Gulf Stream Drift. There were only cold currents far south.

Darkness in winter fell soon after 4 p.m. and there were sometimes inches of snow on the decks; the very rigging became sheathed in ice. It was then that many a poorly-nourished infant died. Their bodies, stitched in canvas, were consigned to the sea after a brief service, while the ship raced on. With a good wind blowing a clipper master did not stop for burial of the dead nor pleas of the terrified living.

When a ship was becalmed in the tropics—and most were—conditions became equally inimical to health. Dr Francis Workman, a surgeon superintendent, wrote that in the doldrums his ship had averaged only forty miles a day. "The vertical sun shining through the misty atmosphere on the glassy ocean—the air saturated with moisture—the ventilation was imperfect (so that) the atmosphere became something I shuddered to go into."

But at least tropic evenings gave opportunity for relief in dancing and concerts on deck. Diaries kept by the more literate passengers tell of Scots, Irish and Welsh emigrants singing songs of home and dancing their national dances.

From such diaries one gains an impression of remarkable resilience among those normally cooped below. Death and fear and acute discomfort might be their lot, but whenever the weather gave them opportunity, they were quick to entertain themselves.

It was made easier for cabin passengers. If the ship were becalmed the officers might take some of the gentlemen by boat a decent distance from the ship so that they could swim without offending the susceptibilities of the ladies. On less favourable days they might engage in shooting

Ships' masters and officers of the Loch Line, photographed in Melbourne.

at bottles suspended from the yard arms, or go "fishing" for birds. Even steerage passengers could join in the "sport" of hooking an albatross, drawing the great bird to its doom. And there was often fishing of the usual kind which sometimes provided welcome variation in a lucky passenger's menu.

On Sunday it was customary for the surgeon superintendent, if there were no clergymen travelling, to take Divine Service. The capstan was covered then with a Union Jack, and from it

Cape Wickham lighthouse on the northern end of King Island, built in 1861, the tallest tower in the southern hemisphere. "The light at Cape Wickham can only be regarded as a beacon warning navigators of danger, rather than a leading light to a great thoroughfare"— Admiralty Sailing Directions.

A chronometer and a sextant –navigation instruments from the Science Museum, Melbourne, of a type used in the immigrant sailing ships. Invented in 1765, the chronometer is a very accurate clock mounted on gimbals to keep it level when the ship rolls. The sextant was evolved from Hadley's quadrant, and first designed in 1757.

a lengthy sermon was read or delivered to those who chose to attend. Most, it seems, did—dressed in their better clothes. Their minds were much occupied with their vulnerability on the remote seas.

"Grant I beseech you health and strength to those who command this frail ship to attend to their respective duties", wrote Nathaniel Levi in his diary in 1853, while far south in the *Matilda Wattenbach,* " and extend thy Omnipotent hand to shield and protect my Dr. (Dear) Mother, Father, Brothers, Sisters-—" They were far behind, perhaps never again to be seen.

On weekdays, classes were held to teach both children and adults to read and write. Debates were another common form of whiling away the super-abundant time, and also many auction sales. Articles auctioned might have belonged a few days earlier to a person buried at sea, one whose bereaved spouse had to eke out family resources.

More often articles were auctioned to pay for gambling debts, for gambling at cards seems to have gone on night and day. Many men gambled away everything they possessed and reached the colony destitute, deluding themselves that they would pick up easy gold.

All of these shipboard activities were at the mercy of the sea. Officiating clergy, auctioneers and teachers alike were sometimes precipitated by a sudden wave among those gathered around them.

In calmer weather the more daring young men might climb the rigging in attempts to reach the masthead, and always in quiet corners, there was opportunity, at least for cabin passengers, to indulge in mild encounters with the opposite sex. One cabin diarist remarked that every young woman seemed to have her head resting in a young man's lap, begging him to sing to her.

But for single men and women travelling steerage, there could be no mingling of the sexes, for they were segregated at either end of the ship, the married couples accommodated between them. A seemingly prudish precaution, but one that experience in the unsegregated days had proved necessary. Emigrant girls travelling alone had become the prey not only of male passengers, but of the very officers who were supposed to protect them.

In the tropics, when dancing under the moon was done, steerage passengers retired below to their foetid quarters. The padlocked lamps were normally put out by ten for the passengers were required to rise at 6 a.m.

Many of the young men took their palliasses on deck, preferring to sleep there, little caring if sudden tropical downpours doused them. If this happened there would be a rush for tubs to catch the rain, as it provided pleasant change from sea water for washing clothes and bathing.

"Lay aloft and furl!"

'Bully' Forbes

The 2600-ton Schomberg, *wrecked at Peterborough on her maiden voyage in 1855. It ruined the career of her master, 'Bully' Forbes. The ship's main mast was 210 feet high, and it carried 3.3 acres of sail.*

*I*t was when the tropics fell behind and the ship turned to "run her easting down" that the capabilities of the masters were tested. Of all the masters of the Golden Decade, none surpassed in achievement and colour the famous 'Bully' Forbes, a man who was to ruin his career on the Otway coast. But before disgrace came, his records stunned the world. On Forbes' death, John Towson was to describe him as the greatest of the masters who had put the theory of great circle sailing into practice.

In the *Marco Polo,* a 1622-ton Canadian-built ship, Forbes sailed from Liverpool in 1852 with 930 emigrants for Melbourne. Until then the run had usually taken three months or more; the record—to Adelaide—stood at 76 days.

Forbes sailed out in 68 days. So great was the excitement in Melbourne that newspapers did not think it untoward that there had been 53 deaths on the voyage; after all, only two had been adults, and births had made good the *Marco Polo*'s numbers.

But while Forbes was racing back around the Horn to England, a ship with even greater losses entered Port Phillip. In December 1852 the *Ticonderoga,* 90 days out from Liverpool with a total complement of 672, had lost 100 lives through an outbreak of typhus.

Her medical supplies had been exhausted; her surgeon was not expected to live; 300 aboard were ill. Most of her survivors were held at a site near Pt Nepean that had been set aside for a quarantine station. No quarantine building had yet been raised. Shelter was improvised from the ship's sails, and huts belonging to local lime burners were taken over. At this site, 70 more deaths occurred.

This tragedy, climaxing as it did losses on earlier ships, moved the Victorian authorities to seek a limit of 350 passengers per ship. It was advice not always heeded, but Forbes and many other masters did not again carry such excessive numbers.

The month after the *Ticonderoga* sailed into Port Phillip, Forbes brought the *Marco Polo* back into the Mersey. He had returned in five months and 21 days—so fast a round trip that the owners thought he had put back through trouble encountered on the outbound voyage.

Forbes was next given command of the *Lightning* and in it set a return Melbourne-Liverpool record of 63 days, a time Lubbock believes was never surpassed by sail. A vivid picture of travel to Australia with him is given in the diary of John Fenwick, who came out to Melbourne in the *Lightning* in 1854.

"The Captain says we must set every yard of canvas, and if that does not make her go, we must put up our shirts." As the *Lightning* carried 13,000 square yards of sail, it will be seen that Forbes was determined on maximum speed.

One of the passengers thought "we ought to petition the Captain to keep up less sail, for he sees very little difference between frightening a man out of his wits and killing him outright." But Forbes was not to be deterred. Two days later, Fenwick was recording: "More sail set and we tear away as if we are to be strained to pieces . . . Now and then a batch of passengers pitched over to leeward—some thrown out of their berths."

Farther south they went:

. . . the ship seems to be going faster than ever—absolutely flying from under one— and every now and then dashing into a sea with a shock that makes every plank tremble . . . When the weather is fine and the sea calm, the Lightning is a very large noble ship—everything about her looks large. In a storm what a change— she is then like a little boat and you can see every bit of her at once, and, as she falls into a sea, you see a great mountain rolling away past . . .

One of Forbes' passengers, on his second *Lightning* voyage, William Greenhalgh, wrote of another side of the famous captain's make-up. A third-class passenger brought pea soup "similar to dishwater" to him. When he began to complain about it Forbes was "much annoyed and said he would put the man in irons if ever he took such a liberty again." But then a whole group of third-class passengers banded together to take up the issue. "They placed their cans in a row when the ship gave a tremendous roll on one side and sent cans of soup and passengers rolling first on one side then the other, all amongst the pea soup (which) spoiled all their clothes (and) caused fine fun and laughter."

Wallowing in spilt foodstuffs was no uncommon experience. Most of the lower classes still carried a good deal of their own food to supplement the dreary, inadequate ship's supplies.

Reports are common of treacle, pepper, sugar and sauces cascading over them as they lay wet and seasick. The din of metal plates, pannikins and cutlery rolling about the floor, vied with the roar of waves across the deck.

'Bully' Forbes' career was ruined in 1855 in a perplexing wreck. Given command of the 2600 ton *Schomberg,* Britain's proud reply to the American-built clippers, he became obsessed with an ambition to reach Melbourne in her in 60 days. Although the *Schomberg*'s mast was 210 feet high, and she carried 3.3 *acres* of sail, she was beset by calms and Forbes seems to have been piqued by the fact.

On Boxing Day, in good weather, land was sighted well west of Cape Otway. That night, when told by his officers he was close to land, Forbes at first did not so much as come on deck, but continued playing cards with the surgeon and an 18-year-old girl.

When he did appear, he stood watching the gap between ship and shore narrowing while all hands waited for his orders. He gave none until it was too late to execute them. The great ship almost beached herself on the spit that juts into Newfield Bay near the present town of Peterborough. All passengers were safely taken off by two passing coastal vessels, but the bulk of their luggage was lost and the beautiful ship was doomed. Within a matter of days heavy storms pounded the pride of Britain to pieces.

Forbes' international reputation seems to have intimidated the colonial courts. Despite damning evidence, he was exonerated because the reef was not charted, but he was never again given a first-class command.

*A body was buried
on the beach at
Mutton Bird Island.*

*Supposed point from which
Tom Pearce rescued
Eva Carmichael.*

*Te
Only re
was*

*This area was full of dense scrub
and inaccessible.*

*The cemetery where Mrs
rmichael, her daughter Raby,
ır Mitchell and Reginald Jones
were buried.*

*Cave.
ed by sea, it
idy and
?.*

*Loch Ard Gorge today. At the top of the
picture is Mutton Bird Island. The Loch
Ard struck to the left of the tip
of the island as seen in the picture.
"Pieces of rock from the cliff face.
dislodged by the yard-arm, were now
crashing on deck..."*

The Great Britain *was one of the first sailing ships to augment wind power with steam on the passage to Australia.*

The Challenge of Steam

Sailing ship masters of this time were well aware that they were competing not only against each other but also against the growing challenge of steam.

Isambard Kingdom Brunel's 3500-ton *Great Britain* made her appearance on the run to Australia in 1852 carrying 630 passengers. Built as early as 1843 she was the first iron-built ocean-going vessel to be equipped with a screw. She also carried 10,000 square yards of sail and depended mainly on these to make speed before the westerlies. But unlike ships dependent entirely upon sail, she used her screw to pass through the doldrums. This meant that she could generally outstrip the passage times of all her competitors.

By 1875, when she was withdrawn from service to Australia, she had completed 32 passages with a fastest time to Melbourne of 55 days, 17 hours.

But she was in a class apart, far ahead of her time both in size and passenger-carrying capacity. And even she was largely dependent on sail.

Although the magnificent *Schomberg* had been lost through carelessness of an inexplicable kind, most masters wrecked at the western entrance had been prevented by poor weather from taking noonday sights before they sought the Otway landfall.

It was much debated whether a Cape Wickham light should also be installed. Some believed that a light there might be mistaken for Otway and so would lead a master to manoeuvre himself into danger instead of out of it.

At all events, no lighthouse was built at Cape Wickham until the Golden Decade was done. The west coast of King Island became one of the worst graveyards of ships in the world.

In 1854 alone, two ships, the *Brahmin* and the *Waterwitch* were lost there after long voyages. But not until 1859 did the Admiralty accept that there was need for a light there. It was finally erected in 1861. Even then, *Admiralty Sailing Directions* were emphatic: "The light at Cape Wickham can only be regarded as a beacon warning navigators of danger, rather than a leading light to a great thoroughfare."

"The ladies on deck"
From Graphic, *June 29, 1872, artist's impression on board the emigrant ship* Indus, *about to sail for Australia.*

From Graphic, *June 29, 1872, artist's impressions on board the emigrant ship* Indus, *about to sail for Australia.*

"The bachelors in the 'tween decks"

"Specimens of the crew"

Because of the low elevation of King Island, the lighthouse constructed was a very high one: 145 feet. Located as it was in the path of violent westerlies it was constructed on massive lines: the walls were 11 feet thick and its foundations went 30 feet into the earth.

To differentiate from the flash of Cape Otway, the Wickham light showed a fixed beam. On clear nights Ford could see it from Otway "as a star with a bright loom." It must have been some comfort to his isolated family to feel that at last their guardianship of the western entrance was shared.

By 1859, the sites of the two lighthouses were linked by the Melbourne-Tasmania telegraph. Unfortunately, the cable repeatedly broke and six months later it was abandoned. The landline to Melbourne remained intact, and was used to pass details of shipping movements.

The Wickham keeper's log gives some idea of the violence of the weather:

July 4th 1863: Dark gloomy weather— Noon. Blowing a tremendous gale, rooting up much vegetation and damaging roofs of cottages. Sunset, gale at its maximum,

being almost a hurricane . . . Lantern vibrating fearfully and the noise of the wind one continued roar. Could not perceive any sign of weakness through the immense pressure on it.

The head keeper, E. C. Spong, was cast in the Ford mould: he remained at his stormbattered post for twenty years.

In 1866 the *Netherby,* another Black Ball Line ship, was driven before storms for a fortnight so that everything on her decks was smashed. She was carrying 452 emigrants and a crew of 50 from London to Brisbane.

It was impossible for her master to take the vital noon observations as she approached the western entrance; indeed, after such appalling weather, he was most uncertain of his whereabouts.

Soon after dark on 14th July, his ship struck the west coast of King Island. All of the boats except one were damaged as soon as they were launched.

By means not recorded, someone managed to get a line ashore. The one remaining boat was drawn back and forth along it and, incredibly, everyone was saved. But still no one knew on what shore they had been cast.

"Live provisions"

While abundant local game kept them alive, the second officer, who appears to have been a most resourceful man, led a party of six passengers northward along the coast. After four days they sighted the tall Wickham lighthouse. Spong immediately prepared to receive the survivors, but he had no means or communication with the mainland. The *Netherby*'s second officer, despite his fatigue, resolved to cross Bass Strait in the station whale boat. Taking four men with him, he reached the mainland coast near Torquay and, at Roadknight's sheep station, broke the news. As a result the Victorian government sent two steamers to King Island for the survivors.

No one did more for Australian-bound emigrants, particularly for young women, than did the saintly Caroline Chisholm. Through the Emigrants' Friends Society which she founded, she put an end, in the ships she controlled, to the disproportionate use of passenger space.

Instead of running three and four class ships, she eliminated classes altogether; also she did everything in her power to help families emigrate and be accommodated together on board. She established a finance scheme to help emigrants raise money for fares—£12 for adults, £6 for children under 14; she greatly improved the dietary scale; she forbade alcohol which frequently exacerbated quarrels among cooped-up passengers. It is a matter for wonder that this woman, aided by a devoted husband, was able to do so much for the poorer classes when those controlling Britain were so little moved by their deprivation.

Unfortunately, the ships under Caroline Chisholm's scheme were relatively few in number; moreover because the Southern Indian Ocean was master of all, suffering was inseparable from the race eastward. As late as 1878, when sail's era was closing, Dr Lightoller the *Scottish Bard* wrote:

> *Talk about shipping water! Solid water in great heavy masses every now and then comes over and fills her up to the bulwarks, and then swills and rushes about like a mill stream. I have just come up on the poop, where a heavy sea has struck the women's bathroom, and broken it into small pieces like match-wood.*

Worse followed:

> *I never saw such a sea in my life; the water is sweeping clean over the vessel; we have only four sails set and it is as much as we can stagger under. The people below are in a deuce of a funk; singing hymns and praying is the order of the day.*

A few days later:

> *Even in the cabin all is wet—clothes, bedding etc. The sickness is beginning to increase again among the children. This is owing to the excessive damp and want of ventilation, for we cannot open the hatches or the people would be simply drowned. There is now about five in. depth of water in the married people's quarters.*

"The galley and the black cook"

*Eva Carmichael (right) with her mother (centre)
and her younger sister Rebecca (Raby), photographed
shortly before the family left Ireland. The bodies of
Mrs Carmichael and Raby were washed into the gorge;
they were buried in the cliff-top cemetery above it.*

It was in the financial interests of ships' masters and surgeons to bring as many emigrants through the voyage as possible for they were paid a bounty on each safely landed. But it says more for human fortitude than for masters' and surgeons' solicitude that the vast majority of emigrants survived. Victoria gained 453,000 of them in the decade between 1851 and 1861 alone.

A very humane young surgeon of one of the last sailing ships to bring emigrants to Sydney, was Dr R. Scot Skirving. This was in 1882. Although only 24, Skirving was a master mariner as well as a doctor. Writing years later of his voyage on the *Ellora,* he leaves no doubt that, even at that late date, the journey was a harsh experience for the majority of passengers.

I must admit that it was horrid, and even indecent for decent married people to be herded together like beasts, with almost no privacy to dress or undress, and where, in the close stuffy bunks they slept in, only a thin board separated each couple from another alongside, another below, and another lot end to end . . . The single men were shut off forward by themselves and berthing was good enough for them. The same thing may be said of the single women's quarters which were in the 'tween decks right aft, totally shut off from the married quarters . . . married couples slept in bunches of 16 human beings in two tiers. I think the very young children slept with their parents and the older children piled in together somehow in double bunks.

The voyage of which Dr Skirving was writing took 120 days from Plymouth to Sydney. One can imagine with what excitement such long-confined passengers smelt the strange, fresh aromatic scents of the Otway Forest when they made their landfall. Anne Bedford, coming out on an unidentified ship in 1864, wrote delightedly in her diary:

A most beautiful morning. We were awakened about 4 o'clock by the shouting of "land". It was Cape Otway about 100 miles from Melbourne and there is a lighthouse on it . . . They have gone very close to it. Our Captain put up many flags. They put up theirs and (told us) they telegraphed from here to Melbourne to let them know of our arrival. They would hear of us four minutes from the time they telegraphed to Melbourne.

Melbourne-bound emigrants put aside the old clothes that most of them favored on the voyage out and donned the best that they had to begin their new life. But it was at this time that the captain had to make his entry to Bass Strait, often with the weather against him. Such was the case of the *Loch Ard*.

Captain George Gibb, 29, master of the Loch Ard *on her fatal voyage. He married a few weeks before the ship departed. "If you are saved, Eva, let my dear wife know that I died like a sailor."*

The Loch Ard

The Loch Ard, *built on the Clyde in 1873. Of 1693-ton burden, she was more than 262 feet long, 38 feet wide, and 23 feet deep. Her masts were nearly 150 feet high. The* Loch Ard *departed Gravesend, Port of London, on her final voyage on March 2, 1878.*

*I*n Victorian folk history the name *Loch Ard* is linked with that of a homestead: *Glenample*. This run was taken up in the 1840s by James Brown. Either he, or James Murray, who purchased it from him, determined the site of the homestead and bestowed the name, though neither appears to have built anything substantial there. Nor was there, in their time, a road linking *Glenample* with the more settled Western District to the north.

Dr Daniel Curdie, a prominent Scottish settler from *Tandarook,* near the present Cobden, blazed a track to the vicinity of Port Campbell. When he saw the magnificent coast, he urged Hampden Shire Council to construct a permanent road. When the road had been formed, the council celebrated its opening with a picnic by the sea. One of the squatters from the Camperdown area, Peter McArthur, brought a friend along with him, a young fellow Scot, Hugh Hamilton Gibson.

Later Gibson wrote:

> *I . . . was taken by the look of the country, and the coastal scenery, and made up my mind to buy the run* Glenample.

Although the run was for sale, Gibson could not raise all the capital he needed. He asked McArthur to join him in the venture. This McArthur did, but Hugh Gibson it was, with his rather frail wife, who went to live at *Glenample* in 1866, there to run 10,000 sheep as well as cattle. It is probable that the homestead they built there was designed by Gibson and that the building of it was supervised by him. He quarried the sandstone for it not far from the site.

Twelve years later Hugh Gibson became responsible for directing the rescue action immediately following the wreck of the *Loch Ard*. By that time he had working for him George Ford, son of the Otway lighthouse keeper, a man who was to prove as resolute as his father.

Because the story of the *Loch Ard* reveals so vividly a risk always attendant upon emigration by sail, especially at the Otway landfall, it is related here in some detail. These, the last emigrants lost in the sailing ship era on the approaches to Melbourne, were not many numerically but the fact that such a disaster could still happen so close to their destination caused a wave of concern.

The Loch Line seems to have been extraordinarily ill-fated. Of 25 of its magnificent iron sailing ships, only six escaped disaster. Yet Basil Lubbock wrote of them: ". . . when steam began to cut in they still held on until they were the last of all the sailing ships to continue carrying passengers."

The *Loch Ard* was built in the Clyde in 1873, of 1693-ton burden, she was over 262 feet long, 38 feet wide and 23 feet deep. Her masts were nearly 150 feet high.

She met with setbacks early in her career. On her second voyage she was struck by violent gales near Kerguelen Island and was only able to reach the western entrance to Bass Strait under jury rig, her masts mere stumps. Nearby were two other sailing ships also nearing the end of their voyage—the *British Admiral* and the *John Kerr*, the latter also struggling under jury rig.

The *British Admiral* struck the west coast of King Island with the loss of 79 lives. The other two

A contemporary artist's impression of the wreck of the British Admiral *on the west coast of King Island. A total of 79 people died.*

vessels successfully entered Bass Strait. The *John Kerr* then stood out to sea off Port Phillip Heads in another gale until a tug could tow her in. "The *Loch Ard*," according to George R. Leggett, an authority on sailing ships, "brought up with two anchors holding her off a lee shore at the back of Sorrento." But she survived the voyage.

In 1878 command of the *Loch Ard* passed to Captain George Gibb. By then her two previous masters had died and this was regarded as a bad omen. Gibb was a 29-year-old Scot, a man who was to prove himself a most capable and considerable master.

A few weeks before his departure for Melbourne on the ill-fated 1878 voyage, he had married Miss Annie Carmichael. As far as is known, she was not related to the family who were to make up nearly half of his passenger list.

There were eight members of this family travelling: Dr Evory Carmichael, who was emigrating from Ireland to Queensland because of his health; his wife Rebecca; four daughters, Rebecca (Raby), Eva, Margaret and Annie, and two sons, Evory and Thomas. One older son, William, had already come to Australia. He had run away to sea, but evidently had re-established contact with the family, for he wrote trying to persuade them to come to join him; in fact, to give emphasis to his letters, he set off home to Dublin and was on his way there when the *Loch Ard* departed from London.

The other ten passengers were: Mr and Mrs John Stuckey, and Messrs W. R. Godby, Reginald Jones, Arthur Mitchell, William Patterson, Thomas Pitts, Herbert Ralf, Gerald Robertson and George Yates.

The *Loch Ard*'s crew totalled 36, among them being an apprentice whose name was to become a household word in Australia: Thomas Pearce. By today's standards he was a short young man—five feet five and a half inches—but strong and very fit. Pearce had, in fact, been born Thomas Millett. His father, an engineer, had emigrated from Tipperary, but had died in New Zealand. His mother had re-married, marrying a

sea captain, R. G. Pearce. The boy had been given his step-father's name, but, before he had turned 15, he and his mother suffered a second blow. Captain Pearce was lost north of Townsville in the wreck of the *Gothenburg*.

At 15, young Pearce went to sea on the *Eliza Ramsden*, but the ship did not so much as clear Port Phillip Bay. Near the Heads she struck the Corsair Rock and was lost. Fortunately all her crew reached safety. It was then that Pearce joined the Loch Line.

The 1878 voyage of the *Loch Ard* to Melbourne was uneventful until the approach to the western entrance of Bass Strait was begun. There, on May 31, Captain Gibb encountered a mist which obscured the horizon. Above it he could see the sun clearly enough for his noon sextant sight, but he knew that the angle measured upward from the mist to the sun was considerably less than it would have been could he have measured from the true horizon.

The smaller angle had the effect of making the ship's position appear further south than it actually was. He appears to have allowed a margin for this but not margin enough. As he approached Cape Otway, he was much nearer the coast than he suspected, so near that even without the mist, the bulk of Moonlight Head would have screened the Otway light from his view.

At Cape Otway lighthouse, Henry Bayles Ford was still supervisor, now in his thirtieth year there. He had already written to his superiors in Melbourne: "Sir, I hereby beg leave to inform you that I am now sixty years of age, and that my health is fast failing... I would most respectfully solicit that I may he allowed to retire on superannuation." His request was to be granted later the same year.

The invisible coast, along which Gibb was groping, had been opened to closer settlement during the past 10 or 15 years, and among the settlers were men and women who were to render great assistance after the impending catastrophe. They bore names still known there: Till, Shields, McGillivray, Robertson, McKenzie.

Eva Carmichael

But of the *Loch Ard*'s fifty-four souls, only two were ever to hear these names. On board the ship the passengers were holding an end-of-voyage party, but Captain Gibb, alert to danger, did not attend it. It was over early and the older Carmichael sisters, Raby and Eva, went to bed at midnight. The ship was riding slowly with close watch being kept. Captain Gibb had estimated that he would be within sight of Cape Otway at 3 a.m.; the morning was Saturday June 1. As far as time was concerned, his estimate was accurate. As they drew near their expected landfall, he sent a man aloft every fifteen minutes. At 4 a.m. the haze lifted and he discerned in the starlight high, pale cliffs only a mile off. The man aloft called that he could hear breakers.

To turn a large sailing ship in so confined a space would have been difficult enough had the master had everything in his favour, but the wind was on-shore and there was also a strong on-shore current. From her cabin, Eva Carmichael heard shouted orders as Captain Gibb tried to have the *Loch Ard* put about.

Mistaking them for cries of jubilation at the sighting of land, she ran up on deck. The scene confronting her left her in no doubt of the true situation. She returned quickly to her parents and must have warned them, as Mrs Carmichael had time to dress herself and the two small girls. The boys were travelling second class in a different section of the ship.

Tom Pearce

But then, to use Eva's words, the ship ran with a "fearful, shuddering crash" onto an outlying reef off Mutton Bird Island. The whole of the wooden top deck was torn from the hull and masts and rigging crashed across the ship. The passenger saloon began flooding rapidly.

Raby and Eva ran up a companionway and reached Captain Gibb's post on the poop deck. Realizing that his ship was doomed, he said, "If you are saved Eva, let my dear wife know I died like a sailor." Pieces of rock from the cliff face, dislodged by the yard-arm, were now crashing on deck and distraught passengers and crew members were trying to shelter from them. The sisters were separated when a wave larger than

the rest swept Eva into the sea. It would seem likely that the same wave swept Tom Pearce and other crewmen overboard as they battled to launch a lifeboat.

Pearce was fortunate in that he surfaced near the upturned boat. He got underneath it and pulled out the plug. Although the tide at first took the boat out to sea, he clung on and, as daylight came, he was washed through the narrow entrance of a gorge in a rampart of sheer cliff. When the boat struck a rock projection, he left it and swam towards a beach piled high with wreckage.

Eva Carmichael could not swim—a fact that probably saved her, for she clung first to a chicken coop, then to a spar. Two men, Mitchell

The Loch Ard Gorge, Saturday June 3rd 1978. Nearly two thousand people gathered before daylight, in stormy weather, to commemorate the centenary of the wreck of the Loch Ard *and to honour all those who made the journey to Australia under sail.*

and Jones, at first clung on with her, but after a time they attempted to swim and were lost to her sight.

The current that had borne Tom Pearce's boat now brought Eva's spar into the same gorge. She had already been about four hours in the winter sea. Telling factors in her favor were her great tenacity and her physique—she was five feet eight inches tall and weighed twelve stone.

In the gorge her spar jammed on the same rock projection that Pearce's boat had struck, but as this happened, she caught a glimpse of a figure on the land and screamed for help. Though Pearce was weak from his own struggles and from many abrasions, including a bad cut on the head, he swam out to her through drifting wreckage. It took him about an hour to bring her ashore.

While he had been alone he had found a deep cave, sheltered from the wind, on the west side of the gorge. (During the past half-century a great deal of rock has fallen at the cave's entrance.) To this he half dragged, half carried the girl.

He took me into a wild-looking cave a few hundred feet from the beach and, finding a case of brandy, broke a bottle and made me swallow some, which revived me. He pulled some long grass and shrubs for me to lie on. I soon sank into a state of unconsciousness and must have remained so for hours.

Pearce drank some of the brandy himself and massaged the girl's body with what was left, then he too slept.

When he awoke, Eva was still "in a stupor" and he realised that he must get help quickly. Her only clothing was a saturated nightgown.

He began trying to find a way out of the gorge. An age-old aboriginal route of ascent and descent was known to some of the settlers, but it descended into thick undergrowth. Pearce was barefooted and his feet were undoubtedly soft after life at sea. He chose to climb the central, dividing point of the gorge, probably using wreckage to make a start.

Four of the Carmichaels who died in the Loch Ard wreck— from top: Dr Evory Carmichael, his daughter Rebecca (Raby), and sons Evory and Thomas.

A view of Loch Ard Gorge from the so-called "Tom Pearce's Cave", taken in the 1890s. Note the debris in foreground.
After the wreck of the Loch Ard, *it was said that debris from the*
wreck was piled eight feet high across the gorge. In fact it is believed that this cave was not
used by either of the survivors. They sheltered together in what is now known as
"Eva Carmichael's Cave", on the other side of the gorge.

When I got to the to the top my heart sank, as I could not see anything that indicated settlement. The thought of Miss Carmichael lying in that cave made me make the effort to get help, but having no boots on, progress was slow.

He was only three and a half miles from *Glenample* and, by great good fortune, came upon hoof prints of two of the station horses. These he followed until he was sighted by the riders—George Ford and the 14-year-old William Till, who were out mustering.

The "Warrnambool Standard" reported how Ford had first seen the "much scarred" young man.

Asking him what was wrong, Ford was told that "the *Loch Ard* was lost, with all on board, passengers, captain and crew, except himself and a girl he had assisted to rescue."

The horsemen rode to *Glenample* for help while Pearce made his slow way back to the gorge. He must have descended by the aboriginal track, for he was found soon afterwards immobilised in the thick undergrowth at its base.

Although Hugh Gibson rode hard to the gorge, it was dark by the time he descended into it. He extricated Pearce and they went to the cave. The rough bed was there, but of Eva there was not a

Port Campbell in the early 1890s.

sign. Ford soon joined the search. From time to time the men "coo-eed", stopping to listen for a reply above the sound of the sea. During this prolonged period Gibson sent young William Till back to *Glenample* for lanterns and the buggy. Three men returned with him — Messrs Robertson, Shields and McKenzie.

As they began their descent they heard George Ford shout, "I have found her! " She was huddled in a hollow under a bush, cold and terrified.

The men built a fire on the beach, wrapped her in blankets and gave her coffee. In the cave, Gibson wrote a telegram for Ford to take to Camperdown. It advised the authorities of the tragedy and asked for protection against wreckers.

On the horse he had ridden all day, George Ford set out at midnight to cover forty-five miles over rough bush roads—a remarkable feat for both man and horse. He was away again from Camperdown next morning by 10 a.m., bringing a mounted trooper with him.

In the meantime, Eva had to be brought up out of the gorge in darkness. "It was a good thing", wrote young William Till, "that we had two such hefty men as W. Robertson and W. Shields, otherwise she would not have seen the top of the cliff that night." They reached *Glenample* between 3 a.m. and 4 a.m. on the Sunday morning. It was now over 22 hours since the ship had struck Mutton Bird Island.

Eva Carmichael explained later that, when she had regained consciousness in the cave and had found Tom gone, she had feared that blacks might attack her and so had concealed herself.

During part of the time she was undoubtedly delirious, nevertheless she had heard some of the "coo-ees", but feared they were from the blacks and had not dared reply.

As soon as news of these events appeared in the newspapers, *Glenample* became the focal point of Victoria, indeed of Australia. Newspapermen, officials, sightseers and, inevitably, wreckers, converged on the lonely spot.

The bodies of Mrs Carmichael and Raby were washed into the gorge; also the bodies of Mitchell and Jones. Wreckers stopped at nothing—one was caught in the act of removing a ring from Jones' finger. For every wrecker caught, half a dozen got away with all manner of articles.

Gibson's house and sheds were used to accommodate scores of officials and newspapermen. At the centre of this throng, safeguarded from insistent pressmen, lay the bereaved girl. To help nurse her and to give her company of her own age, Mrs Gibson sent for Jane Shield, an 18-year-old Princetown girl. The two formed a close friendship during the ensuing weeks.

At the gorge a magisterial enquiry was held into the deaths of the four passengers whose bodies had been recovered. Presiding was Gibson's partner, Peter McArthur. When it had ended, the burials were held just west of the gorge, the service being conducted by a Presbyterian Bush Missionary before some 400 people. "Mr

From left, the Loch Katrine, Loch Tay, Hinemoa, Linfield, *docked at the old Geelong wharf.*

McIntyre read a portion of the 15th Chapter of the 1st Corinthians and delivered a short address from the words, 'And the sea gave up the dead which were in it'."

Others of the *Loch Ard*'s dead were seen briefly in the sea below the cliffs, and several in the nearby blowhole. Despite searchers' efforts, the bodies proved beyond recovering.

Only ten days after the wreck, salvage rights to the *Loch Ard* were sold by auction in Melbourne for £2120, to Messrs Howarth, Miller and Matthews. They recovered perhaps £3000 worth of goods from the shore and the sea. This they dragged well up into the gorge, but a southwesterly gale arose and washed most of it out again. The firm then chartered the 98-ton screw steamer *Napier* to work on the wreck, but after her third visit, the weather suddenly deteriorated. She ran for Port Campbell, but was herself wrecked just inside the harbor.

Eva Carmichael in later life. She died in 1934 at the age of seventy-three.

The only item of real value recovered by the salvage company was a porcelain peacock, five feet high, which had been sent for display at the Sydney exhibition of 1879, and the Melbourne exhibition of 1880. It was one of five such peacocks made by Mintons of England in 1851. Carefully packed, it had bobbed safely ashore. Nearly a century after the wreck, it was purchased for display in the "Flagstaff Hill" Warrnambool Maritime Village Museum.

On June 22 Tom Pearce gave evidence in Melbourne at an enquiry into the loss of the *Loch Ard*. It was soon evident that he was as well able to conduct himself in the witness box as he had during the disaster.

Even though his statement is couched in nautical terms that today are little understood, one may recognise in reading it the thorough grip the young man had of his calling. Three or four passages will be quoted from the plainer parts of his evidence.

Captain Tom Pearce in later life. He died in 1909 at the age of forty-nine.

The rescue rocket team at Port Campbell in 1891, at the tragic wreck of the cargo-carrying sailing ship Fiji. *Rockets were used to try to fire lines from shore to ships in trouble.*

It was just as the watch was being relieved at 4 o'clock that land was seen. I think the captain and the man at the wheel saw it simultaneously. Our watch was going below—some had gone—when I heard the order to hoist up the stay sails, and at the same time the captain ran forward, calling all hands on deck. We got sail on her as quickly as possible with a view to bringing her about on the other tack, and as soon as she gathered way the captain gave the order, "All hands ready about." Every man was at that time on deck, but when the helm was put hard down the ship just came up head to wind, and then commenced to fall off again, as there was not sail enough to bring her round. As soon as the captain saw she was beginning to fall off again, he ordered both anchors to be let go. The port anchor was let go first and was immediately followed by the starboard anchor. I should say we were then about half a mile from the shore, and I heard others estimate the distance the same. We were among the broken water.

The anchors dragged, but they had brought the ship head to wind. It was then that Captain Gibb attempted the port tack.

The ship was just gathering way when she struck. I believe the rock made a great hole in her bottom, for she was bumping very heavily. When the ship struck, I heard the captain give orders to have the boats cleared away, and the port lifeboat made ready for the ladies . . . I do not think the passengers could have been got into them, owing to the heavy seas that were washing over the main deck. The seas were coming over both sides, as the back wash from the cliffs was bringing the sea in over the lee side.

Pearce and five others were trying to release a lifeboat. "I cut the after gripe and kicked out the chock, while Smith cut the forward gripe, and just then a sea came on board and washed us all away."

The Chairman of the Inquiry complimented Pearce on his precise and detailed account.

When the evidence was published, the public was in a state of frenzy to see so cool and courageous a young man. People soon had an opportunity at the Melbourne Town Hall, where he was awarded the gold medal of the Humane Society.

The papers claimed that 5000 people managed to jam into the hall. As soon as Tom Pearce appeared "the enthusiasm of the spectators found relief in cheering which lasted five minutes."

A week later, in Sydney, 7000 people attended a similar function. Only three days later, back in Melbourne, he was subjected to a gala concert. When he arrived at this with the Governor, "every seat was taken and over a hundred people were standing."

The Victorian government awarded him £1000 and presented him with an inscribed gold watch; Sydney pressed on him a set of nautical instruments; Warrnambool outfitted him; a schottische was composed in his honor. By then he must have longed to get back to the sea however fearful his experiences.

But the public wanted nothing less than Tom Pearce's marriage to the girl he had rescued. If the sea had cast them up together, then surely they were meant to remain together. Neither of the young people themselves appear to have thought so, though there is evidence that Tom Pearce felt obliged to propose because, in the terms of the day, he had compromised the girl.

Eva's physical strength and buoyant temperament helped her to recover. Three months after the wreck, Tom Pearce was among those to see her off from Port Melbourne for her return to Ireland, the Victorian government having paid her passage. Not surprisingly she chose a steamship for her return.

The two young people never saw each other again and only briefly corresponded.

In 1884 Eva married Thomas Achilles Townshend, who was born at Castle Garrycloyne, near Blarney. Tom Pearce had by then married the sister of Robert Strasenbergh, a fellow apprentice lost on the *Loch Ard.* When he died in 1909, at the age of only fifty, he had long been a master in steam ships. He had two sons, both of whom had gone to sea. One pre-deceased him, perishing as an 18-year-old apprentice on the *Loch Vennachar,* lost with all hands off Kangaroo Island in 1905. The other, Robert Strasenbergh Pearce, went on to an award of the DSC in the First World War, only to die in the Second when the freighter *Wairmarama*, of which he was master, was lost with nearly all hands during a dive bombing attack. It had been carrying aviation fuel to Malta.

Eva Townshend died in 1934 at the age of 73 at her home in Bedford, England. A death notice appeared in the Melbourne "Argus"; " . . . Mrs Townshend was the Eva Carmichael who, with the late Tom Pearce, were the only two survivors of the ship *Loch Ard . . .*"

The gorge into which Eva Carmichael and Tom Pearce were washed more than a century ago soon became known by the name of their ship. Perhaps it was Victorian morality that segregated the young couple into separate caves whenever their story was told. The cave they shared became "Eva Carmichael's Cave". Tom Pearce's name was given to another cave in the eastern arm of the gorge.

As the years passed, people forgot where the *Loch Ard*'s remains lay. There were many searches for her, particularly after the Second World War, when scuba diving became popular. In 1967, after long study of the evidence, the Warrnambool diver Stan McPhee located her. Unfortunately his success was observed and, soon afterwards, plundering of the wreck's remaining cargo began. Even explosives were used.

The Commonwealth Receiver of Wreck, who had been advised by McPhee of his find, intervened. Two hundred pigs of lead were recovered from a farm near Cobden, but thousands of dollars worth of both lead and copper had already been taken and sold.

Four years later, working on advice from local fishermen, McPhee went on to locate at Peterborough the remains of the only other emigrant ship lost on the Victorian side of the western entrance: 'Bully' Forbes' *Schomberg*. Strangely, a large part of the *Schomberg*'s bows had drifted as far away as the South Island of New Zealand. A section retrieved there was identified by the builders in 1871.

In 1932 the death occurred in Victoria of Jane Osborne (nee Shields), the Princetown girl whose companionship had helped Eva Carmichael back to health. As she herself had wished, she was buried near the Carmichael grave above the Loch Ard Gorge.

By then a number of pioneer graves were clustered on that windswept spot. But the year after the wreck, when the wayward William Carmichael, only surviving son of the family visited there, only one grave existed. Over it stood a cross made of spars from the wreck, placed there by Hugh Gibson. William Carmichael arranged to have erected the tall stone that may still be seen there:

"Shall Not the Judge of all the

Earth do Right "

Sacred

to the Memory of

Mrs Evory Carmichael

and

Miss Raby Carmichael

Whose Bodies lie Beneath

Also

In Remembrance of

Dr Evory Carmichael

Misses Margaret and Annie

Carmichael

Master Evory and Thomas

Carmichael

All of Whom were Lost in the

Calamitous Wreck

of the "Loch Ard"

Saturday, June 1st, 1878

This Stone is Erected by

Eva and William Carmichael,

The Former of Whom was most

Miraculously Preserved,

In Affectionate Remembrance of

Their Deceased

Parents, Brothers and Sisters

The stone raised, William rejoined his ship, the *Loch Ness* of which he was chief officer. Later a second stone was erected to the two men who had briefly shared Eva's spar:

In Memory

of

Arthur Mitchell

and Reginald Jones

Who Lost Their Lives

In the Wreck

of the Loch Ard

1st June 1878

The Closing of an Era

By sail Victoria was founded, and for 40 years sail brought most of her immigrants.

What was the cost in ships and lives? The number of lives lost might never be accurately known, for reports of wrecks are not always specific on the point. But it is known that 26 ships bringing emigrants to the Australian colonies were lost . . . lost by errors of navigation, by fire, by collision with other ships, and with icebergs. All that can be said with reasonable certainty is that over 2000 emigrants carried in them perished as a result of these wrecks.

The loss of 368 emigrants on the *Cataraqui* was equalled by losses from the *Strathmore* in 1875; both were exceeded by the *Guiding Star* in 1855. It is believed that the *Guiding Star* was "embayed" . . . forced by the wind into a bay within an iceberg 40 miles long. Her 480 emigrants were never heard of again.

But such losses were exceeded by deaths from disease on the long journey out. During the eight busiest years of Victorian gold rush—1852 to 1859—a total of 1307 Melbourne-bound emigrants alone were buried at sea.

If the overall story of losses could be told, the case of the *Loch Ard* would appear a relatively minor one.

Nevertheless, occurring when it did where it did, and leaving only two young survivors, it gained a niche in the State's history. It occurred when Australians were beginning to feel that the risks attending the journey from the Old World had almost passed: the Suez Canal had already been opened for nine years; the Orient Line was about to put a 5400-ton steamship on the run. And it occurred only a few hours out of Melbourne, at the very landfall that had been regarded by sailing men from earliest times with trepidation.

To us, over a hundred years later, the wreck epitomises the risks taken by all those who emigrated under sail.

Happily, nearly all arrived safely, though for few was the voyage an easy one. It is fitting now that we honour them, the men who brought them, and other people, like Caroline Chisolm and Henry Bayles Ford, who brought safety to their landfall.

A dramatic photograph aboard a sailing ship in heavy seas. Note the relationship of mast and horizon line.

the owners, Gibbs, Bright, and Co., Liverpool; or to Geo. Seymour, Sun-court, Cornhill, London.

TEMPERANCE LINE of PACKETS from LONDON to AUSTRALIA.

—Passage money £18 18s.—For GEELONG, Melbourne, and Sydney, the new frigate-built ship SAMPSON, A 1, 985 tons register, 1,500 tons burden. This very superior vessel, only recently built, is admirably suited for passengers, having eight feet height between decks, and great breadth of beam. The ventilation will be made most perfect, as in addition to the ordinary appliances, she will be fitted with the ventilating apparatus recommended by Mrs. Chisholm. Baths and wash-houses will be erected on deck, and a library of 300 volumes will be supplied for the use of the passengers. A minister and an experienced surgeon will accompany the vessel. Passage money for single persons and families 20 guineas. A few berths will be let at 18 guineas, for which, however, early application must be made to Griffiths, Newcombe, and Co., 27, Rood-lane, Fenchurch-street, London.

GOLDEN LINE of AUSTRALIAN PACKETS.

—Goods shipped by this vessel will be landed on the wharf by the steam-tug and lighters the owners have provided for the purpose, and being fitted with a steam-engine to work the winches, a discharge in a few days after arrival is insured.—For MELBOURNE, (takes no steerage passengers,) will have immediate despatch, the superb new clipper-ship GUIDING STAR, A 1 at Lloyd's, 2,004 tons o.m., and only 1,475 tons per register, sister vessel to the well-known clippers Star of the East and Miles Barton, which have just made the remarkably fast passages to Melbourne of 76 and 82 days respectively. Will be loaded to the best possible trim, under the special superintendence of Mr. Mitchell (the Surveyor to the Underwriters,) for the express purpose of making the quickest passage on record) an expectation her magnificent model fully justifies; her accommodation for cabin passengers cannot be surpassed. To secure room early application should be made to the owners, Millers and Thompson, 4, Drury-lane, Liverpool; or to Grindlay and Co., 194, Bishopsgate-street, London.

MARSHALL and EDRIDGE's LINE of AUSTRALASIAN PACKET SHIPS.

—The following first-class SHIPS, noted for their fast-sailing qualities, have most superior accommodations for passengers; load in the London Dock, and will meet with immediate despatch:—

Ships.	Tons Register.	Tons Burden.	Destination.
Eliza	912	1,200	Sydney
Nimroud	1,022	1,300	Ditto
Phoenician	521	700	Ditto
Waterloo	700	900	Port Phillip
Lloyd's	1,229	1,060	Ditto
Navarino	493	650	Hobart Town
Abberton	454	600	Ditto
Constance	578	700	Launceston
Prince of Wales	358	550	Ditto
Eva Johanna	649	700	Geelong
Jeannette Philippine	630	700	Adelaide

For terms of freight or passage-money, dietary scales, and any further information apply to the undersigned, who are constantly despatching a succession of superior first-class ships (regular traders) to each of the Australasian colonies.

MARSHALL and EDRIDGE, 34, Fenchurch-street.

Advertisements from a London newspaper during the era of emigration to Australia by sail. Note the reference to the famous Caroline Chisholm in the top advertisement. The glowing terms of the Golden Line advertisement for the Guiding Star *proved unfortunate: the ship is believed to have collided with an iceberg. Her 480 emigrants were never seen again. "He said he was going south as far as possible"—a report of the* Guiding Star's *last signal in mid-Atlantic.*

Photographic proof that the stories of the rigours of life for sailing ship crews were not exaggerated. "The wind . . . seized upon great masses of the roaring peaks—cut them off—and drifted them away."

The British Board of Trade medal
presented to Tom Pearce during the
period of public acclaim following
his heroic rescue. It was discovered
in a Sydney junk shop in the 1950s.

The author expresses his gratitude to Donald
Walker and Robert L. Suggett for their pictorial
research and production work on the original
text to the first edition, and to the following
institutions and individuals for help in gathering
material for this publication. Because of space
limitations the list is not an exhaustive one, but
to the many others who helped, my thanks.

Author's acknowledgements

*La Trobe and Mitchell Libraries, and their staffs,
    for emigrant diaries, ships' newspapers,
    contemporary daily newspapers and
    periodicals.*
Liverpool City Libraries, UK
National Maritime Museum, Greenwich, UK
London Public Record Office
*Australian Medical Association Library,
    Melbourne*
Royal Historical Society of Victoria
Geelong Historical Society
Heytesbury District Historical Society
Shiplovers' Society, Melbourne
Department of Transport (Lighthouse Division)
Shaw, Savill Albion & Co.
Furnes, Withy & Co.
Miss Innes Cameron
Mrs Rosamund Duruz
Mr Colin McArthur
Mr Stan McPhee
Mrs Marjorie Morgan
Mrs E. Pullin
Miss S. A. E. Ström
Captain David Wharington
Mr Donald Walker
Mrs E. A. Walker
Mr T. Wicking

Further acknowledgements

Calendars of Distinction Ltd, London, UK
Mr Peter Williams
Dr John Chapman
*La Trobe Library, State Library of Victoria:
Mr Ross Gibbs, Miss Mary Kehoe*
Royal Historical Society of Victoria
Science Museum of Victoria: Dr H. Downing
Mr John Brown
Melbourne Harbor Trust
Mr Robert Townshend, Suffolk, England
Mr and Mrs D. Hannah

Further Reading

BLAINEY, Geoffrey:
The Tyranny of Distance
Macmillan, 1982

CHARLWOOD, Don:
Wrecks and Reputations
Burgewood Books, 1996
and
The Long Farewell
Burgewood Books, 1998

LONEY, J. K.:
Wrecks Along the Great Ocean Road
Marine History, 1997

WALKER, Donald:
Beacons of Hope
An early history of Cape Otway and King Island
lighthouses
Athelstone Trust, 1998

WELCH, Major J. H.:
Hell to Health; the history of
quarantine at Port Phillip Heads,
Sorrento Historical Society